# Family and friends

# At school

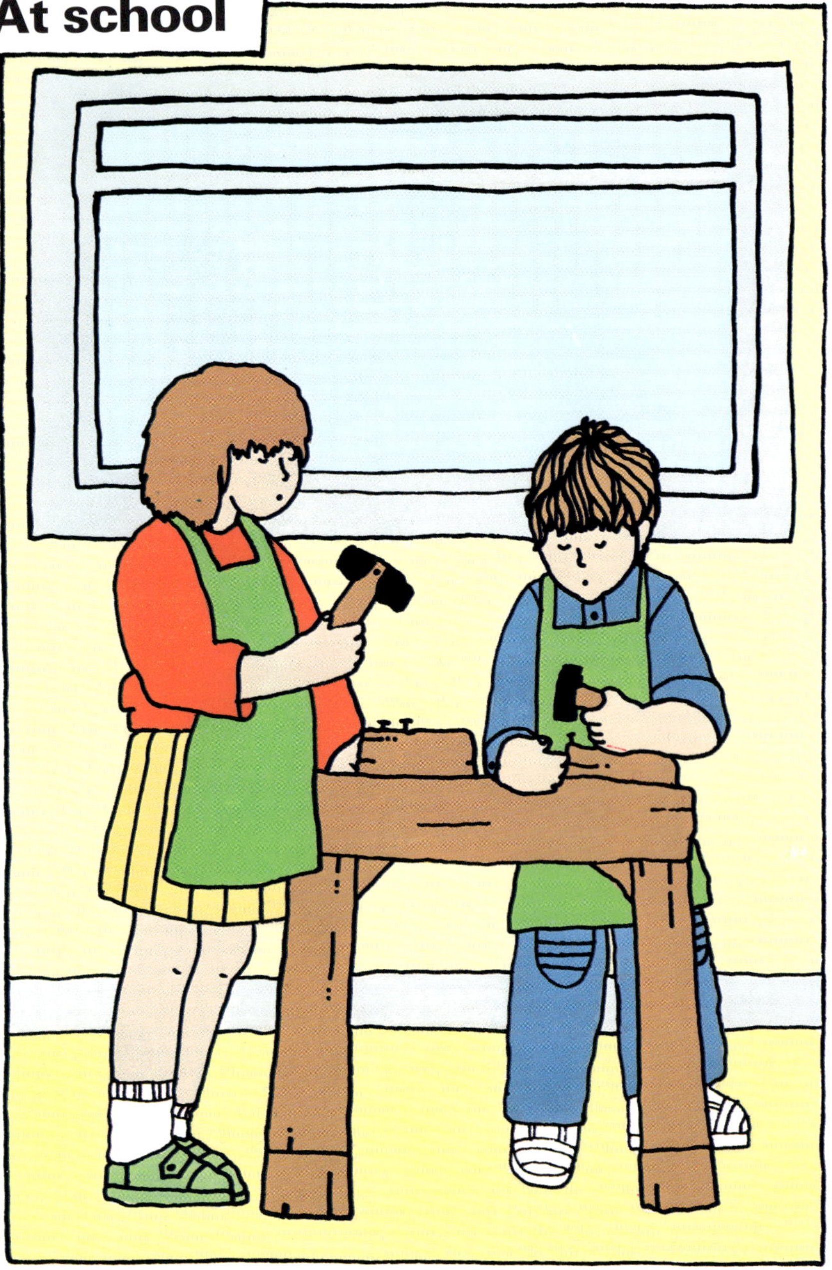

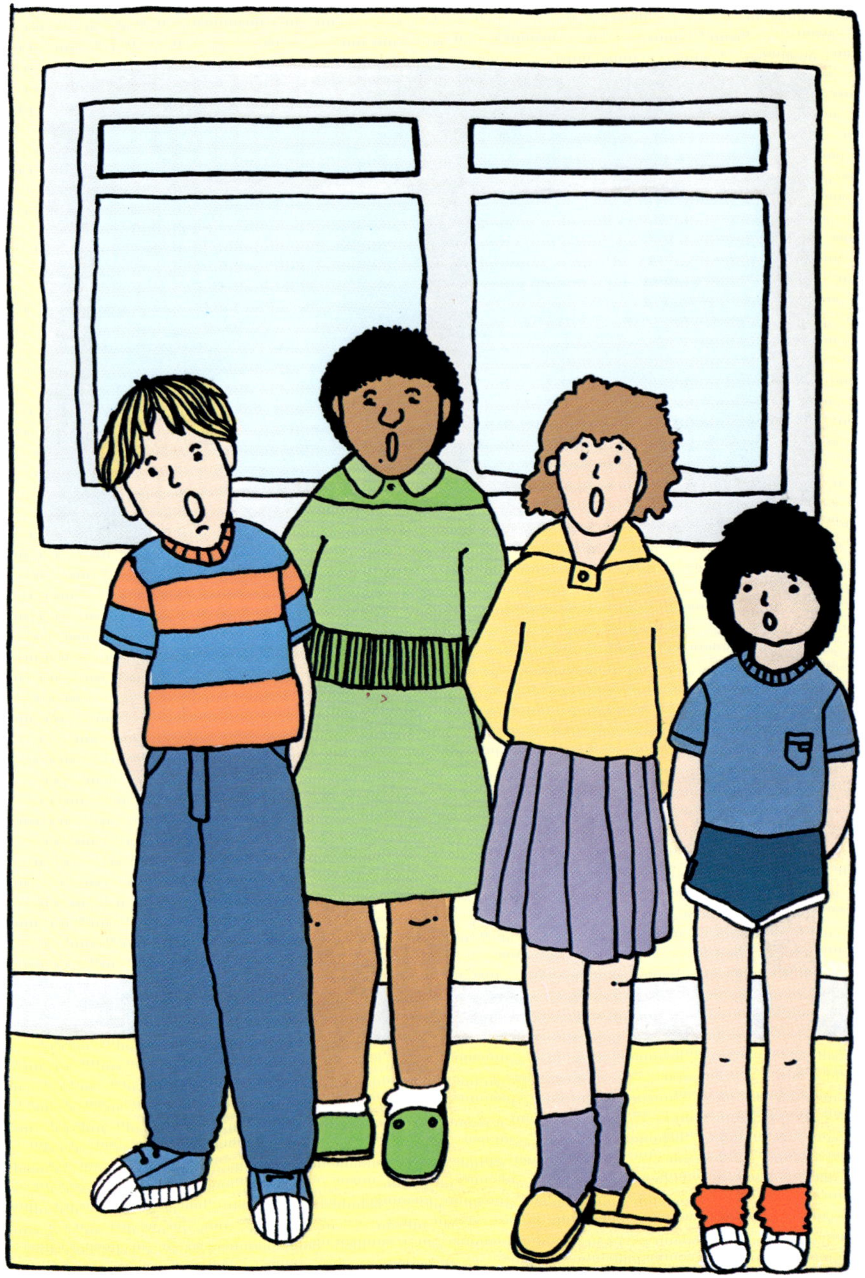

**In the country**

# A windy day

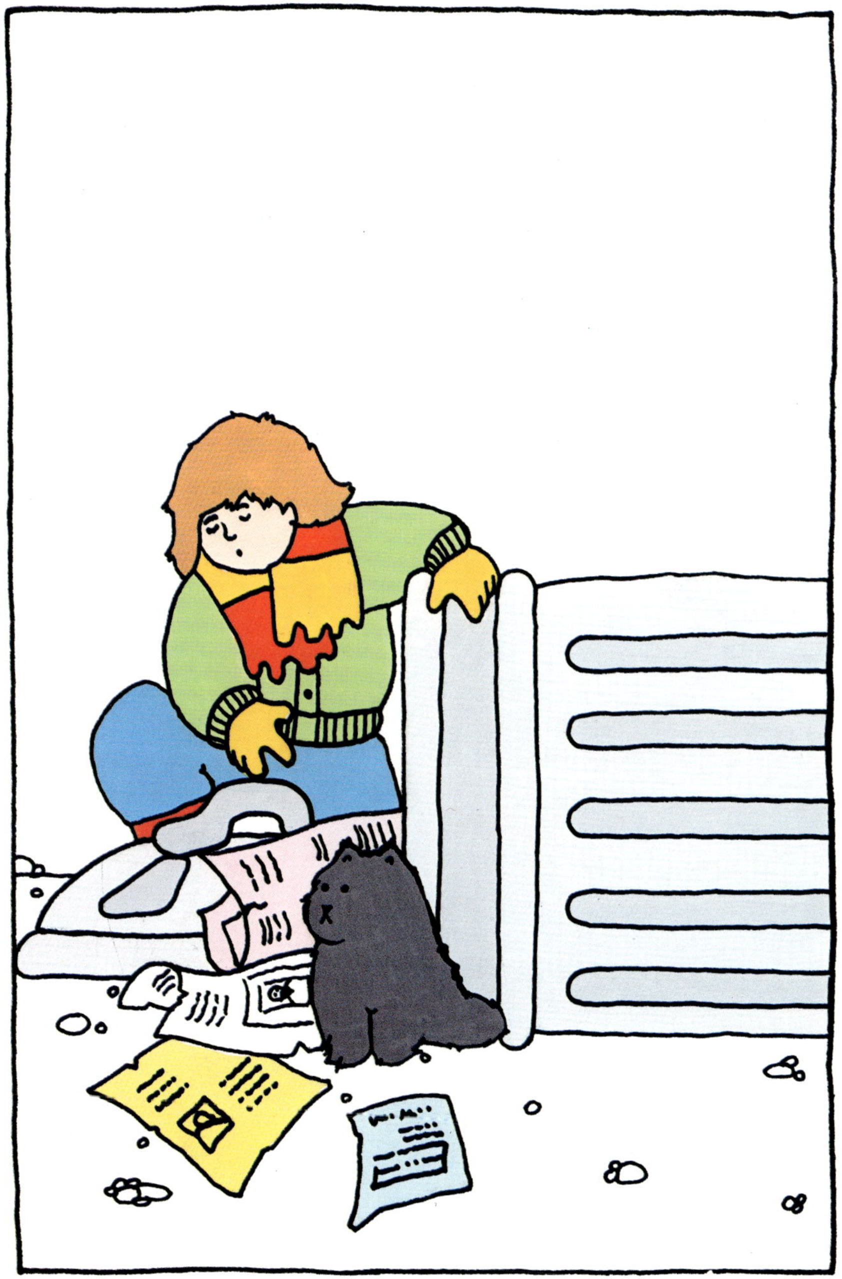

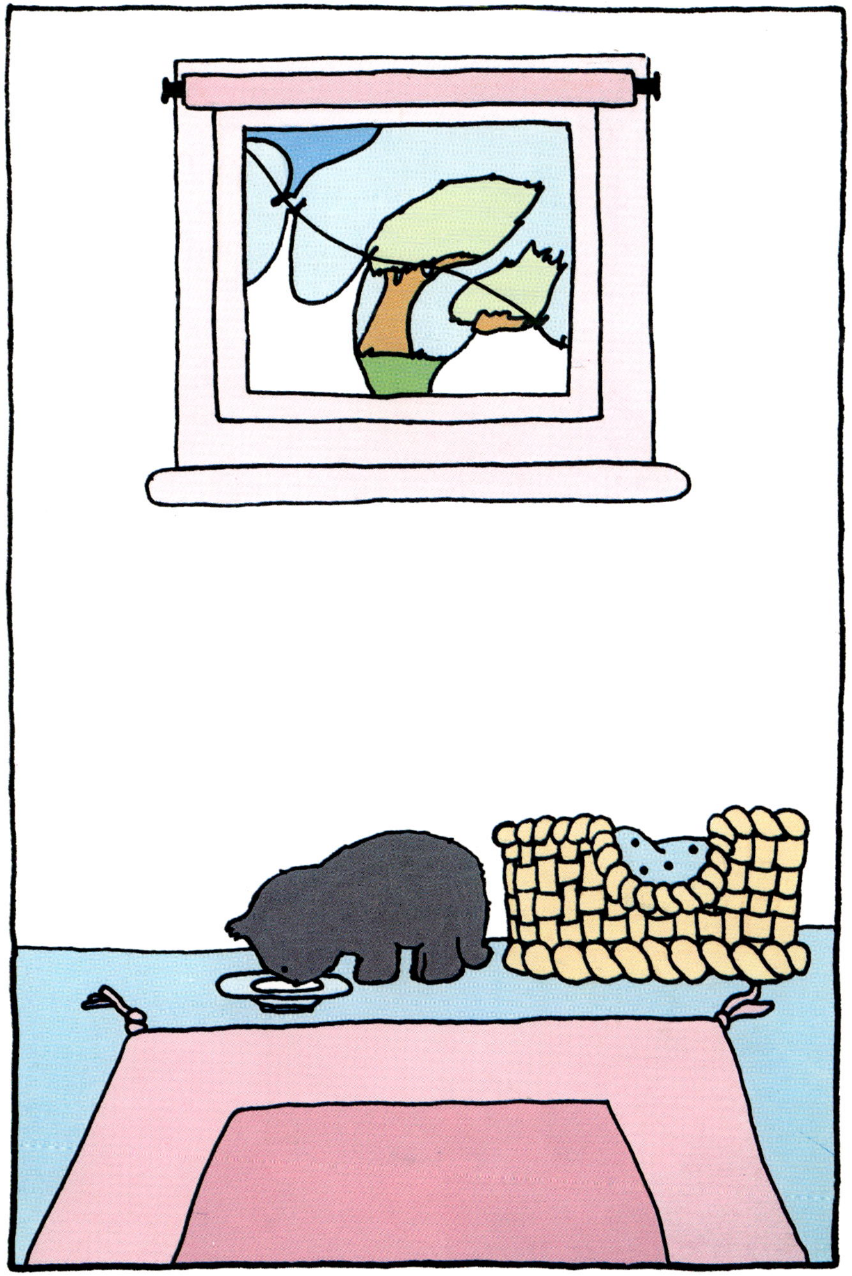

# Music corner

What is your friend playing?

Make the same sound.

Is it loud or quiet?

Now it's **your** turn to start.

# Music corner

Listen to the chimes.
How many times did the chime bar sound?
What o'clock is it?

Now it's **your** turn to play.

# Tea time

# Making sounds

Fill a carton with sand.
Put the lid on. Shake.

Tap a coffee tin with
a spoon.

Tap two pencils
together.

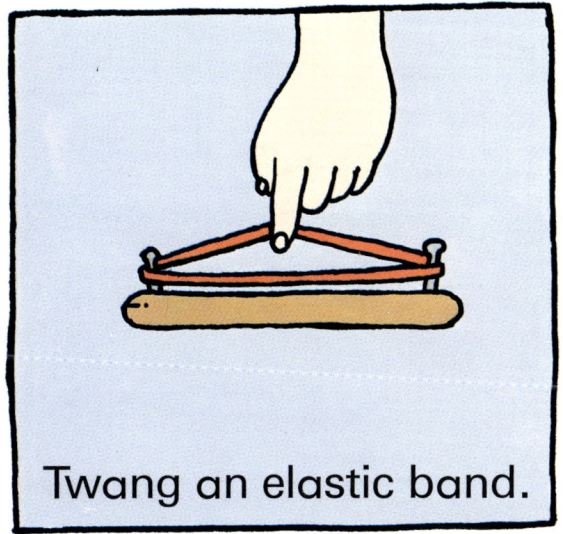

Twang an elastic band.

Rub your sleeve.

Whistle.

What other sounds can you make?

# Making different sounds

How many **different** sounds can you make?

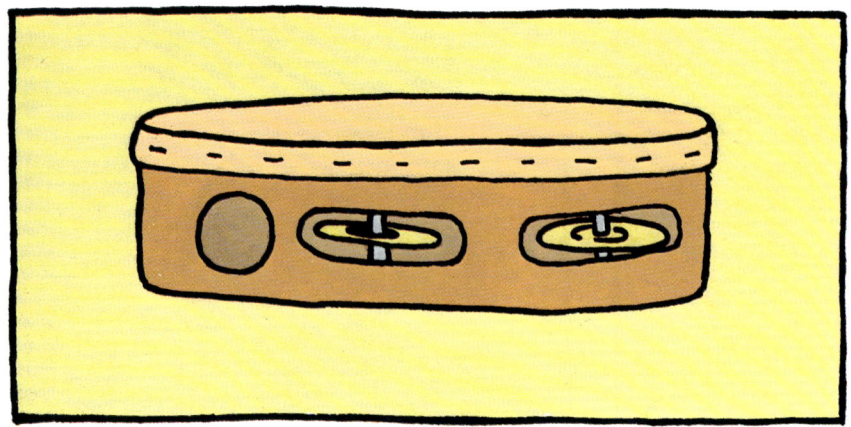

on a tambourine?

on a triangle?

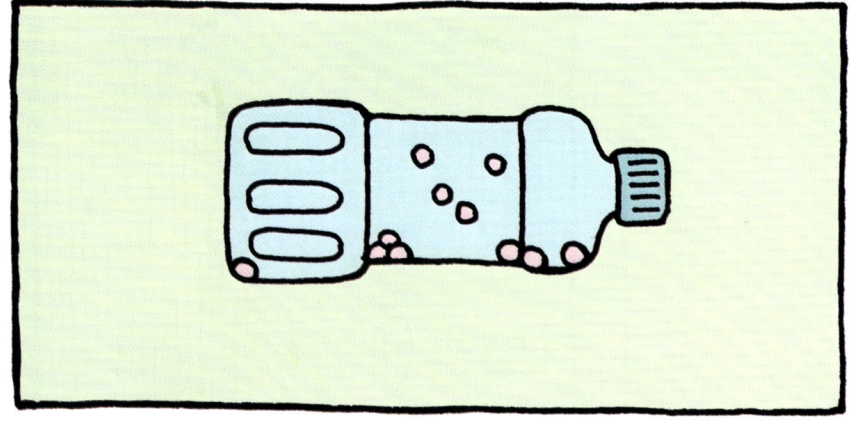

with a shaker?

with a cup and spoon?

# Copy these sounds

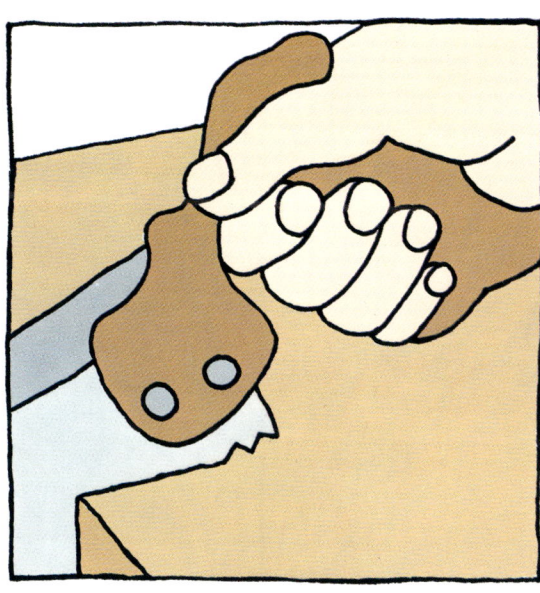

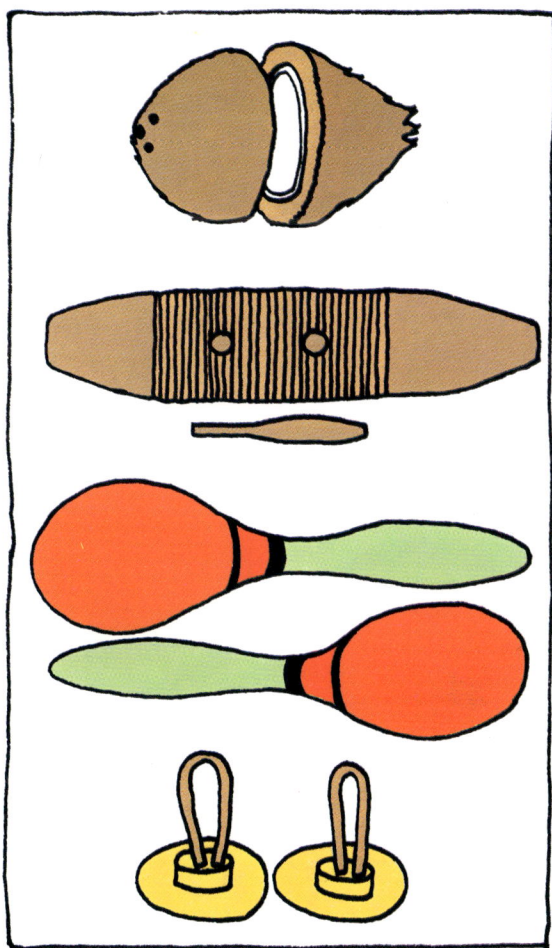

Which instrument will you use?
How will you play it?

# Listen

These pieces of music are all **different**.
Which picture do they fit?

This lady is dancing with clogs on.

Listen out for the **trumpet**.

Listen out for the funny sounds
made by her **clogs**.

This quiet lullaby will help the baby go to sleep.

The **piccolo** is a **tiny flute**.
It plays for these **Chinese dancers**.

Could you dance to this music?

# How did Jane come to school?

How did Jane come to school,
Come to school, come to school?
How did Jane come to school
On this Monday morning?

Show us Jane, if you please,
If you please, if you please,
Show us Jane, if you please,
On this Monday morning.

# Come and dance with me

Come and dance with me,
Come and dance with me,
Round and round and round and round and
Come and dance with me.

Come and skip with me

Come and march with me

Come and sit with me

# Our instrument song

We can play our
rubber drums.

We can play our
castanets.

We can play our
tambourines.

We can play our
jingle bells.

We can play our
shakers.

We can play our
triangles.

# I can hear two soldiers

I can hear two soldiers
Marching down the street.
Left, right, left, right,
Listen to their feet.

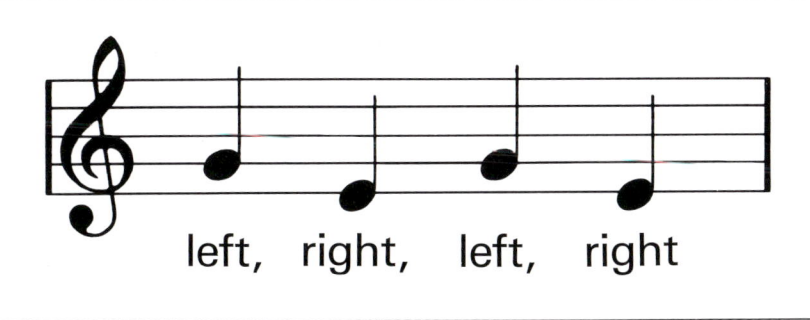

left,   right,   left,   right

four soldiers

six soldiers

eight soldiers

ten soldiers

# Ten little pennies

Ten little pennies sitting in my purse
Ten little pennies sitting in my purse

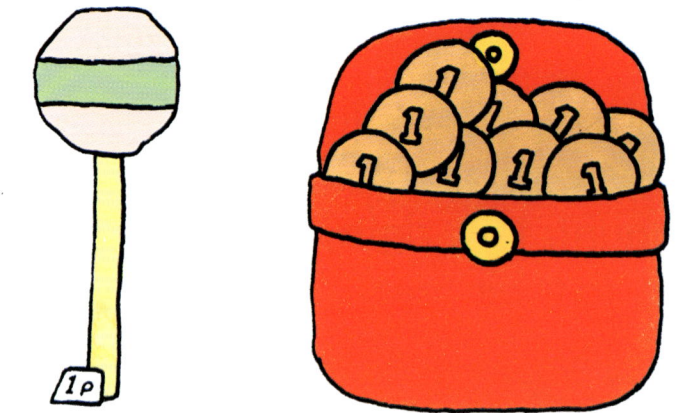

And if one little penny will buy a lollipop,
There'll be nine little pennies sitting
in my purse.

And if two little pennies will buy
a cherry cake,
There'll be eight little pennies sitting
in my purse.

And if five little pennies will buy
a counting book,
There'll be five little pennies sitting
in my purse.

# What can we hear . . . ?

What can we hear when we all wake up,
All wake up, all wake up?
What can we hear when we all wake up,
When we all wake up in the morning?

We can hear the milkman come.

We can hear the postman come.

What else can **you** hear first thing in the morning?

# The little pig

There was an old woman and she had a little pig,
    Oink, oink, oink.
There was an old woman and she had a little pig.
It didn't cost much and it wasn't very big.
    Oink, oink, oink.

Now that little pig curled up in a heap,
He joined his friends and they went to sleep.

The farmer woke them one by one

They rolled and rolled and rolled and rolled

24

# The farmyard

One day as I walked round the farm . . .

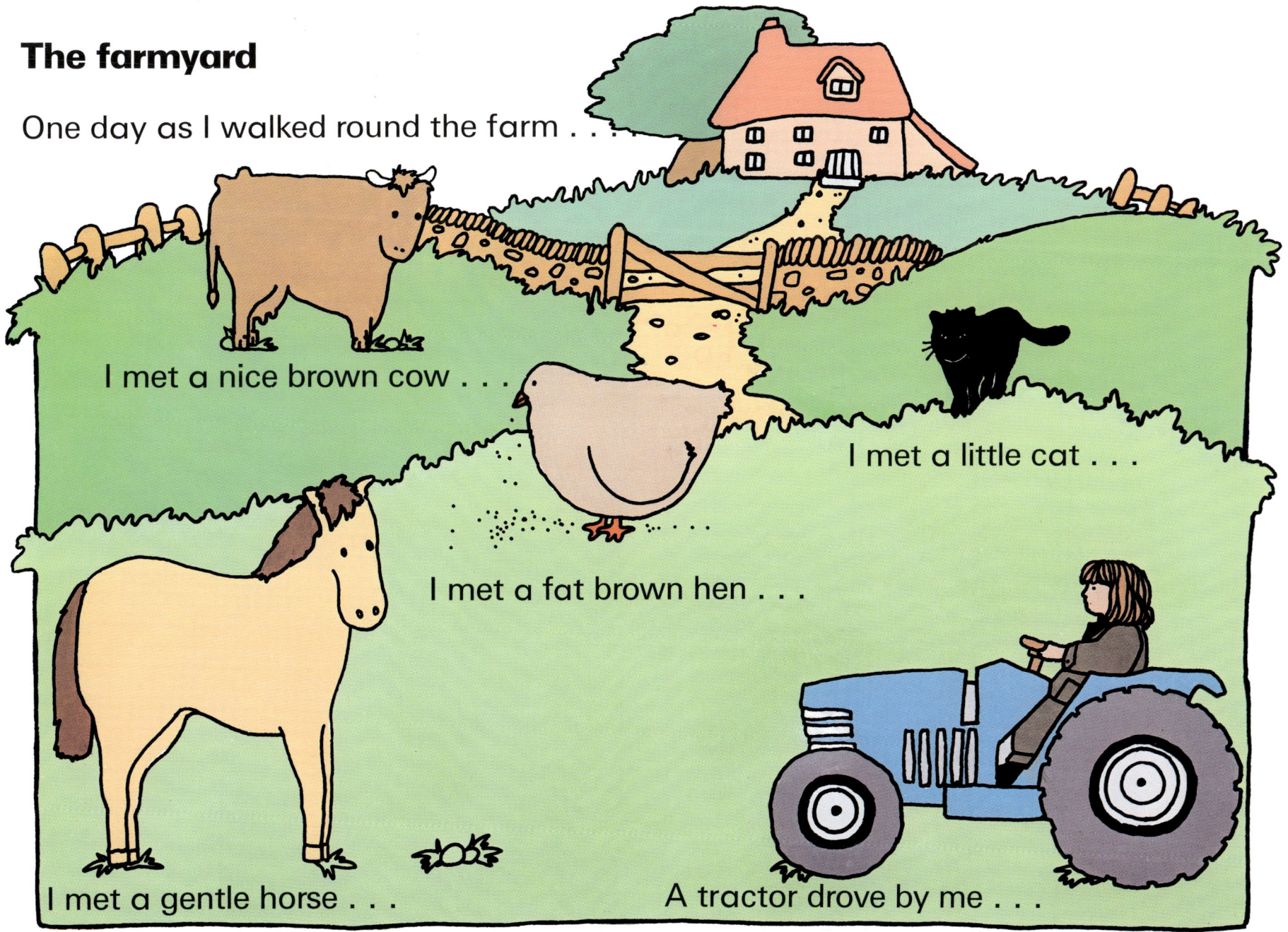

I met a nice brown cow . . .

I met a little cat . . .

I met a fat brown hen . . .

I met a gentle horse . . .

A tractor drove by me . . .

# Colours

I know a man called Mister Red,
He wears saucepans on his head.
I know a man called Mister Black,
He keeps peanuts in a sack.

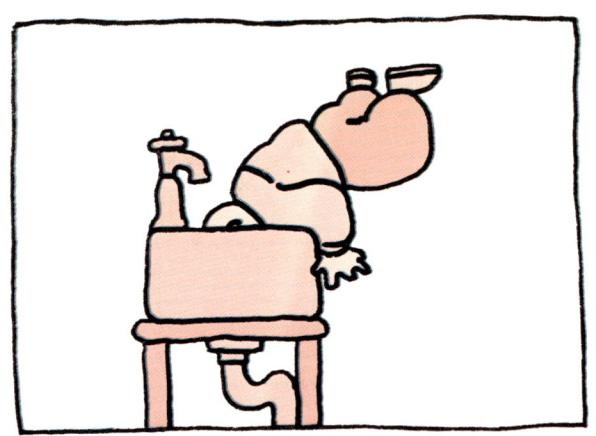

Mister Pink

Mister Blue

Mister Brown

Mister Green

# Five little field mice

Five little field mice fast asleep,
All in a huddle and all in a heap.
A tawny owl came past and gave a
And the first little mouse went scoot!

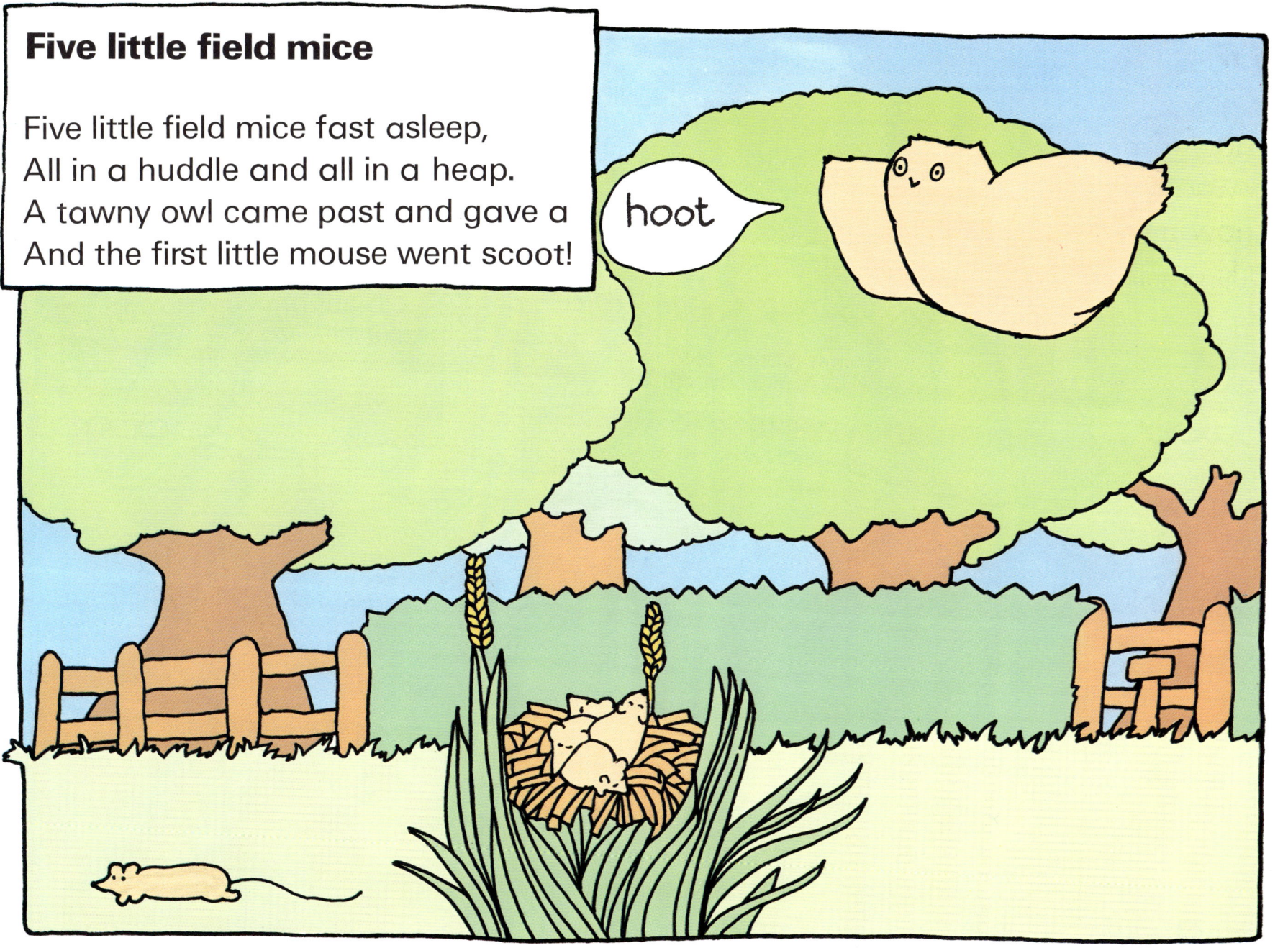

# The wind blows east

Oh, the wind blows east, the wind blows west,
The wind blows the papers right down in town.

Oh, the wind blows the papers right down in town,
Oh, the wind blows the papers right down in town.

## Dancing puppet

See my little puppet,
My puppet on a string,
See him dance round and round
When I pull the string.

Dance little puppet,
Please dance for me,
Dance around and around
For us all to see.

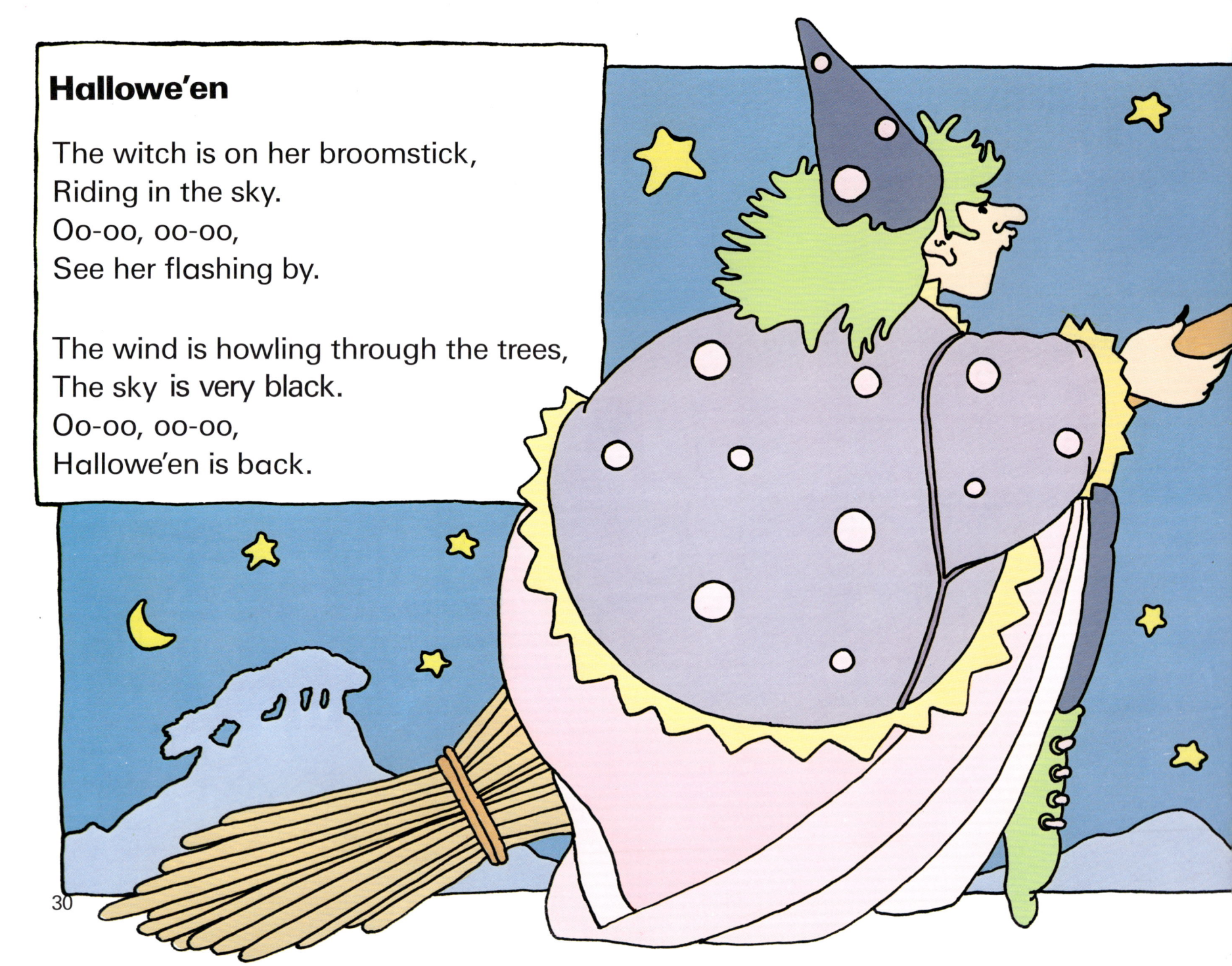

# Hallowe'en

The witch is on her broomstick,
Riding in the sky.
Oo-oo, oo-oo,
See her flashing by.

The wind is howling through the trees,
The sky is very black.
Oo-oo, oo-oo,
Hallowe'en is back.

The goblins dance and jump about
Up and down the street.
Click-clack, click-clack
Go their dancing feet.

The cat is prowling through the grass,
Can you see her eyes?
Meow - meow,
Catch her by surprise!

31

**Lullaby**

Lullaby, lullaby,
Close your eyes my darling.
I will sing a lullaby,
Lull-a-lull-a-by.